Cut-Up Couture

Koko Yamase

KAKKOII KUCYUURU RIMEKU by Kimiko Yamase
Copyright © Kimiko Yamase 2009
Photographs © Osamu Yokonami 2009
All rights reserved.

Original Japanese edition published by EDUCATIONAL FOUNDATION BUNKA GAKUEN BUNKA
PUBLISHING BUREAU.

Publisher of the original Japanese edition: Sunao Onuma
Photography: Osamu Yokonami
Art direction and design: Yoshie Kawamura (otome-graph.)
Styling: Mikiko Ban (CAB)
Hair and make-up: Joji Morikawa (gem) (p. 8-33, 72-85), Nobuyuki Shiozawa (mod's hair) (p. 36-69)
Models: Ai Tominaga, Thaysse Ricci, Doriana, and Karolina J
Editing: Shinobu Ninomiya,

English edition published by arrangement with EDUCATIONAL FOUNDATION BUNKA GAKUEN
BUNKA PUBLISHING BUREAU through The English Agency (Japan) Ltd.

English-language rights, translation, and production by World Book Media, LLC
Email: info@worldbookmedia.com

Translated by Kyoto Matthews
English-language editor: Lindsay Fair

First published in the United States in 2012 by Interweave Press

interweave.com
Interweave Press LLC
201 East 4th Street
Loveland, CO 80537-5655 USA
interweave.com

Printed in China
10 9 8 7 6 5 4 3 2 1

Contents

In this book, we cut and sew everyday menswear—dress shirts, sweatshirts, and T-shirts—into elegant, fun, unique women's clothing. We show that menswear is practical, functional, and inherently elegant. After all, it is made for men who work and play hard, and want to feel good doing it. The classic shapes and silhouettes of these raw materials inspire dozens of creative redesigns.

Even if you are not an expert sewist, you can still have fun making these garments. The designs of some of these pieces almost feel like three-dimensional (and utterly fashionable) clothing puzzles. Enjoy!

Koko Yamase

Sweatshirts
and T-shirts ▶ ▶ ▶ ▶ ▶ ▶ ▶ ▶ ▶

COCO CHANEL first introduced cotton jersey fabric to the fashion world. In this couture redesign, we'll use basic T-shirts and cotton jersey sweatshirts with ribbed cuffs and ribbed hems as our raw materials.

Large and extra-large shirts are ideal for these projects as they offer the most fabric and drape to work with.

Draped Blouse
from Sweatshirt

Starting with an extra-large sweatshirt, accordion-fold the body from the bottom and secure it, front and center. This creates gorgeous butterfly-like drapes.

Instructions, page 10

Tunic
from Twin T-shirts

A chic tunic was created by sewing two T-shirts side by side like mirror-image twins. The wide ribbon accent stabilizes the cut edge.

Instructions, page 11

Draped Blouse

from **Sweatshirt,** *Shown on page 8*

MATERIALS

1 long-sleeve sweatshirt **(Men's XL)**

INSTRUCTIONS

1. Cut off both sleeves, leaving a 1¼" (3 cm) seam allowance at the shoulder seam and gradually decreasing to a ¾" (2 cm) seam allowance at the underarm seam.

2. Fold the raw edge of the armhole over twice and stitch to create a finished sleeve.

3. To create a band, cut off one ribbed sleeve cuff from the sweatshirt. Fold the ribbed sleeve cuff in half lengthwise and sew along the edge. Press the seam open and turn the band right side out.

4. With the seam facing up, attach the short lower edge of the band to the center front of the bodice 3½" (9 cm) below the bottom edge of the ribbed neckline.

5. Make about eight pleats from the bottom of the bodice and wrap with the band. Secure in place by hand sewing the band to the inside of the garment.

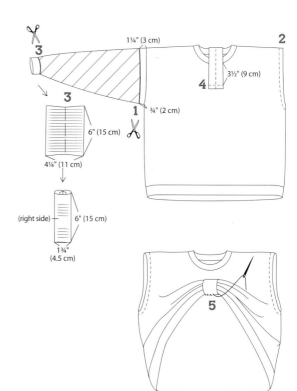

10

Tunic

<u>from</u> **Twin T-shirts,** *Shown on page 9*

MATERIALS

2 short-sleeve T-shirts **(Men's L)**
2 ½ yards (220 cm) velvet ribbon [1½" (3.8 cm) wide]

INSTRUCTIONS

1. Cut the two T-shirts. Make sure that the cut is made on the inner edge of the ribbed neckline.

2. On the left bodice, fold the raw edge over ⅜" (1 cm) to the right side. Press. Cut a piece of ribbon to the length of the folded edge. Align the ribbon with the fold and topstitch to the left front bodice.

3. With right sides together, match the raw edges of the back bodices and sew together.

4. Overlap the front bodices to replicate the original shape of the neckline and approximate T-shirt dimensions (see illustration 4). Starting and stopping 3" (7.5 cm) from each shoulder seam, sew ⅛" (0.3 cm) from each edge of the ribbed neckline, sewing through all layers.

5. Fold the remaining piece of ribbon in half and attach at the neck overlap by sewing through one layer of ribbon. Tie in a bow to finish.

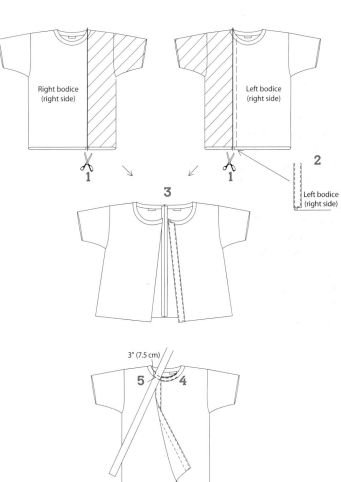

Bustled Frock Top
from T-shirts

The bustle effect is created from a
couple of strategically placed rogue
sleeves. Gather up the fabric of an
extra-large T-shirt and sew it to a
smaller fitted T-shirt.

Instructions, page 14

Bustled Frock Top

from T-shirts, *Shown on page 12*

MATERIALS

1 short-sleeve T-shirt **(Women's S)** (For a larger-sized finished garment, begin with a larger-sized women's T-shirt)

1 short-sleeve T-shirt **(Men's XL)**

2 yards (180 cm) velvet ribbon [¾" (2 cm) wide]

INSTRUCTIONS

1. Using Template #1, cut the smaller T-shirt into a bodice with a curved lower edge. To position the template, lay the T-shirt flat with the side seam facing up. Place the template's center front fold line on the center front of the T-shirt and the template's center back fold line on the center back of the T-shirt.

2. Using Template #2, cut through the front layer only of the larger T-shirt. Cut a 2¼" (6 cm)-wide semicircle through the back layer only. This will become the skirt portion of the garment.

3. Sew two rows of gathering stitches across the raw edge of the larger T-shirt. With the right sides together, align the two T-shirts at center front, matching A with a (see illustration 3). Adjust the gathering stitches to align the two shirts at center back, matching B with b (see illustration 3). Sew together.

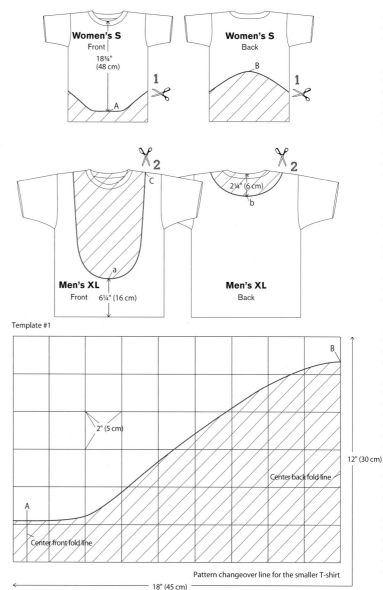

Women's S Front
18¾" (48 cm)
A
1 ✂

Women's S Back
B
1 ✂

✂ 2
C

✂ 2
2¼" (6 cm)
b

Men's XL Front
6¼" (16 cm)
a

Men's XL Back

Template #1
2" (5 cm)
A
Center front fold line
Center back fold line
12" (30 cm)
Pattern changeover line for the smaller T-shirt
B
18" (45 cm)

4. Turn the garment right side out and topstitch the ribbon in place.

5. Use extra fabric to make the sleeve cuffs (see illustration 5). With right sides together, sew along the shorter edge to create a tube. Sew gathering seams around the tube edge. Adjust the gathers to fit the sleeve and sew the cuff onto the sleeve. Fold the raw edge of sleeve cuff over twice and stitch to create a finished hem. Repeat this step for the other sleeve.

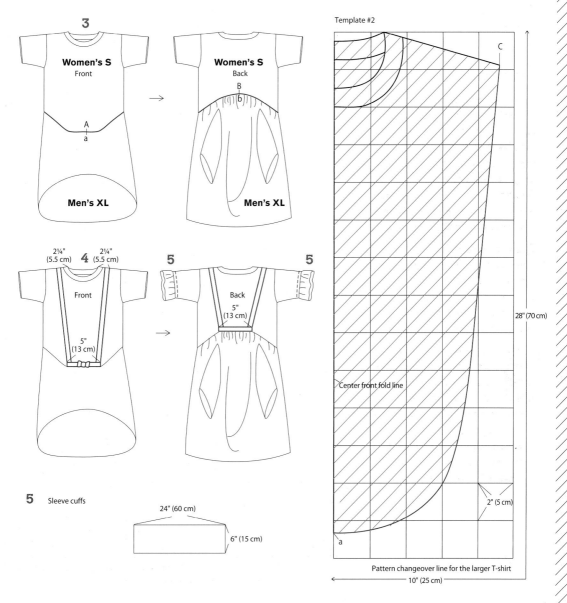

Template #2

3

Women's S
Front

A
a

Men's XL

Women's S
Back

B
b

Men's XL

2¼"
(5.5 cm)   **4**   2¼"
(5.5 cm)

Front

5"
(13 cm)

5

5

Back

5"
(13 cm)

5"
(13 cm)

C

28" (70 cm)

Center front fold line

2" (5 cm)

a

5   Sleeve cuffs

24" (60 cm)

6" (15 cm)

Pattern changeover line for the larger T-shirt

10" (25 cm)

Blouse with Flutter Sleeves *from* Sweatshirt

These light, butterfly-like sleeves cap generous cutaway armholes, making an easy-breezy summer fashion.

Instructions, page 23

Balloon Top from Sweatshirt

Cut a sweatshirt open like you're slicing a hide into a rug. Instead of a bearskin, though, you're sewing with soft (and humane!) jersey. Sew it up into a tube, leaving openings just for arms and a ribbon.

Instructions, page 18

Balloon Top

from Sweatshirt, *Shown on page 17*

MATERIALS

1 long-sleeve sweatshirt **(Men's L)**

2¼ yards (200 cm) satin ribbon [1½" (3.8 cm) wide]

INSTRUCTIONS

1. Cut the bodice side seams and sleeve seams open.

2. With right sides together, align (A) with (a) (see illustration 2), and sew bodice back and left sleeve together to (C).

3. With right sides together, align (B) with (b) (see illustration 3). Sew bodice front and the left sleeve together with a seam that measures 4¾" (12 cm) from the hem. Stop stitching and leave a 2" (5 cm) opening for the ribbon. Resume stitching for 5" (13 cm). The remaining part of the seam will be left open for the armhole. Repeat steps 2 and 3 for the right side of the garment.

4. Fold the raw edge over ⅜" (1 cm) around each armhole. Press. Topstitch on the right side of the garment.

5. Topstitch around all edges of the ribbon openings. Thread the ribbon through the openings and tie in a bow to finish.

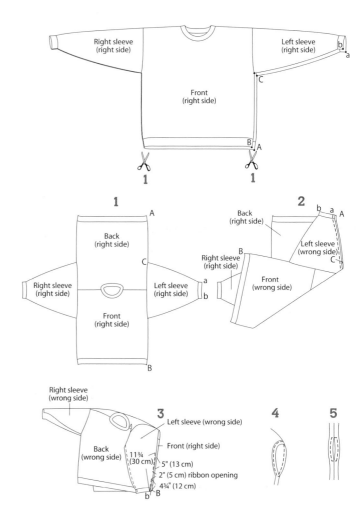

Sculptural Dress with Deep Collar

from Sweatshirts, *Shown on page 32*

MATERIALS

1 long-sleeve sweatshirt **(Men's L)**
1 long-sleeve sweatshirt **(Men's XL)**

INSTRUCTIONS

1. Cut the sleeves and neck of the L-sized sweatshirt. Make sure that the cut extends below the ribbed neckline at center front.

2. Turn one sleeve inside out and sew the end closed. Turn the sleeve right side out and tuck it into the armhole opening to create a pocket. Repeat this step for the other sleeve.

3. Fold the raw edge of the neckline over twice and stitch. Make a $1\frac{1}{4}$" (3 cm) pleat at the center front neckline and at the center back neckline. Press.

4. Cut the bodice of the XL-sized sweatshirt.

5. Cut open the side seam 7" (18 cm) from the cut edge. Fold the raw edges over twice and stitch.

6. Make two bands from the remaining ribbed sleeve cuffs (see illustration 6). With the seam facing up, attach the short upper edge of the band to the center front of the bodice $\frac{3}{4}$" (2 cm) below the neckline. Attach the second band to the center back of the bodice in the same way.

7. Slip the piece sewn in step 5 onto the piece sewn in step 3 (see illustration 7). Wrap the bands up and around the piece sewn in step 5 and hand sew in place. Pull the piece sewn in step 5 upwards to create the dress bodice.

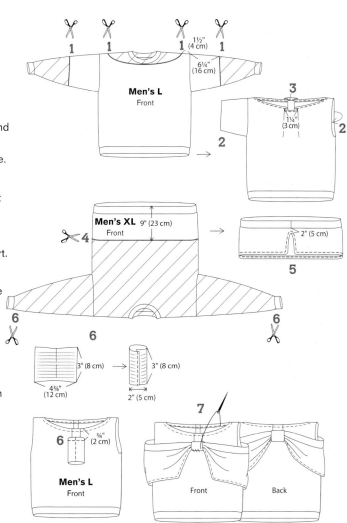

Blouse with Buttoned Shoulders from Sweatshirts

This roomy boatneck blouse with epaulet-style buttons and gathered dolman sleeves has multiple identities. Wear it as a skirt (see photo, top right, on page 21), or wear it upside down as sarouel pants (see photo, bottom left, on page 21). The only difference? How you button your buttons.

Instructions, page 22

Blouse with Buttoned Shoulders
from Sweatshirts, *Shown on page 20*

MATERIALS

3 long-sleeve sweatshirts **(Men's L)**

10 buttons [$^3\!/_4$" (2 cm) in diamerter]

$^3\!/_4$ yard (70 cm) elastic tape [$^1\!/_4$" (0.7 cm) wide]

INSTRUCTIONS

1. Cut all three sweatshirts 14$^1\!/_2$" (37 cm) from the bottom hem.

2. Cut the left side seams of sweatshirts A and B. Do not cut the side seam of sweatshirt C.

3. Sew buttons onto the ribbed hem of sweatshirt A (see illustration 3). Make sure all buttons are spaced equally from the center. Make matching buttonholes on sweatshirt B.

4. With right sides together, sew sweatshirts A and B together at both side seams.

5. Sew gathering seams on the raw edge of sweatshirt B. Adjust gathers to fit the raw edge of sweatshirt C, then sew the sweatshirts with right sides together.

6. Make a small slit in the ribbed bottom hem and thread the elastic tape through. Stitch the ends of the elastic tape together and hand sew the slit closed. The garment is complete.

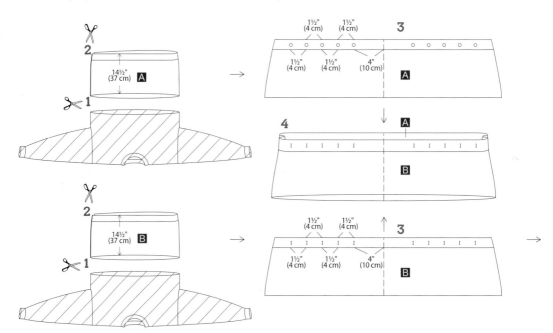

Blouse with Flutter Sleeves

from **Sweatshirts,** *Shown on page 16*

MATERIALS

1 long-sleeve sweatshirt **(Men's L)**

INSTRUCTIONS

1. Cut off the sleeves.

2. Fold the cut end of one sleeve inside out at the armhole seam. Cut the top layer into a curved shape, then cut the bottom layer into a curved shape ¾" (2 cm) longer than the top layer. Repeat for the other sleeve.

3. With right sides together, sew the sleeves onto the armholes.

4. Fold the raw edges of the underarms over twice and sew with the elastic thread on the wrong side of fabric (see page 87) to finish.

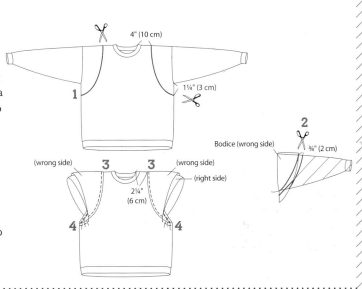

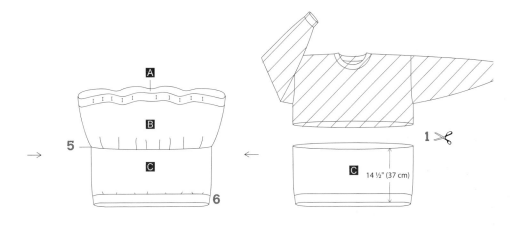

Evening Coat
<u>from</u> Sweatshirts

Stack two different-sized sweatshirts
lengthwise in a simple, elegant design.
Sew a pleat along the back hem and
you are ready for a night on the town

Instructions, page 26

Capelet from Sweatshirts

Have you ever seen a sweatshirt look so cute? The sweet, clever yoke is created from a cut and grafted neckline with its ribbed hem still attached.

Instructions, page 27

Evening Coat
from Sweatshirts, *Shown on page 24*

MATERIALS

1 long-sleeve sweatshirt **(Men's L)**

1 long-sleeve sweatshirt **(Men's 2XL)**

1 button [1¼" (3 cm) in diameter]

INSTRUCTIONS

1. Cut the neckline and sleeves of the L-sized sweatshirt to create the bodice.

2. Cut off the bottom of the sweatshirt 15¾" (40 cm) from the shoulder.

3. Working with the front layer only, cut the sweatshirt open at the center. Cut ⅝" (1.5 cm) from both sides of the center front. Trim the corners into rounded edges at the neckline.

4. Cut the 2XL-sized sweatshirt. Working with the front layer only, cut the sweatshirt open at the center front. This will become the skirt.

5. With right sides together, sew the remaining portion of one sleeve together along the raw edge, stopping at the armhole. Tuck the fabric into the armhole opening to create a pocket. Repeat this step for the other sleeve.

6. With right sides together, align the bodice and skirt at the center front and side seams. Secure with pins. Make pleats on the front and at center back, so the bodice and skirt align evenly. Sew.

7. Fold the center front edges and neckline over twice and stitch. Repeat this step for sleeve openings.

8. Create patch pockets from the remaining fabric and sew onto skirt.

9. Make a buttonhole. Attach button near the collar to complete the coat.

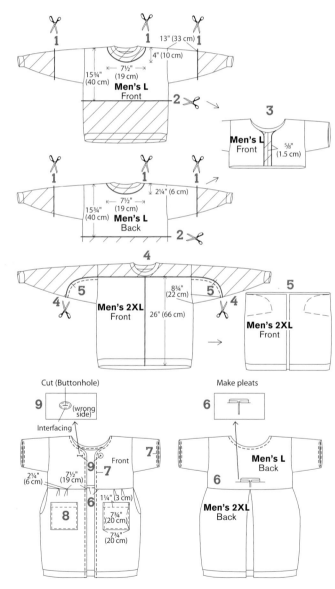

Capelet

from Sweatshirts, *Shown on page 25*

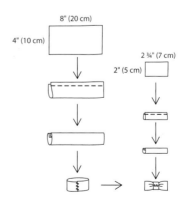

MATERIALS

2 long-sleeve sweatshirts **(Men's L)**

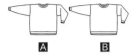

INSTRUCTIONS

1. Cut sweatshirt A. This will become the yoke.

2. Cut sweatshirt B. This will become the bodice.

3. With right sides together, align the ribbed hem of the bodice with the curved raw edge of the yoke and stitch together.

4. Fold the raw edge of the bodice bottom over twice and stitch to create a finished hem.

5. Use the remaining fabric to make a bow (see illustration 5). Sew the bow to the center front of the capelet to finish.

> This cape can be made using just one sweatshirt, but we used two different-colored sweatshirts for a two-tone look.

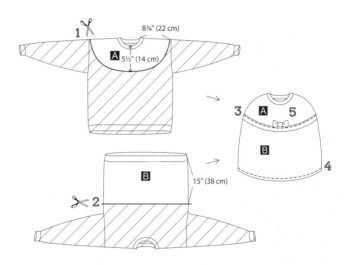

5 How to make a bow

Inside-Out Blouse
from T-Shirt

Aha! Pull the t-shirt bottom through the neck opening to create a ruffled collar. What a treat!

Instructions, page 30

Trompe l'oeil Jumper
from T-Shirt

Cut open the shoulder of a big T-shirt
and attach the ribbed collar to a tank
top. It truly tricks your eyes into seeing
layers.

Instructions, page 31

Inside-Out Blouse
from T-Shirt, *Shown on page 28*

MATERIALS

1 short-sleeve T-shirt **(Men's L)**
11¾" (30 cm) velvet ribbon [1½" (3.8 cm) wide]

INSTRUCTIONS

1. Make 10½" (27 cm) cuts at the T-shirt side seams, approximately 5½" (14 cm) from the bottom hem (see illustration 1). These will become armholes inside the blouse.

2. On the right shoulder, align the two "a" points and sew to create a dart. Repeat this step on the left shoulder.

3. Turn the bodice bottom to the inside and pull it through the neck opening.

4. Stitch around the neckline just below the ribbing (see illustration 4), making sure to separate the T-shirt front and back while sewing. Fold down excess fabric to create a gathered collar.

5. Attach ribbon underneath collar at center front to finish.

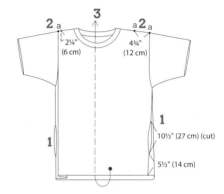

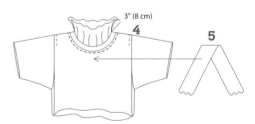

Trompe l'oeil Jumper

from T-Shirt, *Shown on page 29*

MATERIALS

1 tank top **(Women's S)** (For a larger-sized finished garment, begin with a larger-sized women's T-shirt)

1 short-sleeve T-shirt **(Men's XL)**

2 ¼ yards (200 cm) velvet ribbon [1½" (3.8 cm) wide]

INSTRUCTIONS

1. Cut the shoulder seams of the T-shirt. Fold the raw edges over twice and stitch.

2. Turn one sleeve inside out and sew the end closed. Turn sleeve right side out and tuck into the armhole opening to create a pocket. Repeat for other sleeve.

3. Slip tank top inside the T-shirt (see illustration 3). Hand sew the tank top to the ribbed neckline of the T-shirt, making sure to stitch through the front layers only. Repeat hand sewing for back layers.

> **For a belted look, tie the ribbon around the waistline.**

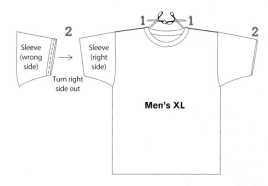

Sleeve (wrong side) Turn right side out Sleeve (right side)

Men's XL

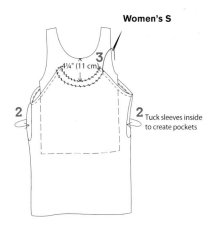

Women's S

4¼" (11 cm)

Tuck sleeves inside to create pockets

Sculptural Dress
with Deep Collar
from Sweatshirts

Classic style, hypermodern design:
This little black dress is made from two
sweatshirts.

Instructions, page 19

Strapless Top with Bow from Sweatshirt

The enormous decorative bow is made from a cut sleeve and pulled through a ribbed band. Traditionalists, listen up: sports gear really can be turned into elegant designs.

Instructions, page 86

Men's Shirts ▶▶▶▶▶▶▶▶▶

There's a reason the "boyfriend" shirt is a
perennial favorite in a girl's wardrobe. It's
roomy, cozy, and just a little sexy. With the
projects in this book, see the myriad ways
men's shirts can be cut up and restyled,
just for you. Even collars, cuffs, and button
plackets become stylish accents in these
new constructed pieces.

Ruffled Dress from Men's Shirts

Here we play with the curved bottom edge of a men's shirt and turn it into a billowy, flirty detail. Pleated sleeves double as neckline ruffles.

Instructions, page 38

Blouse with Kimono Sleeves <u>from</u> Men's Shirts

This kimono-sleeved top makes brilliant use of front button plackets. Shirt collars are crafted into shoulder accents.

Instructions, page 39

Ruffled Dress
from **Men's Shirts,** *Shown on page 36*

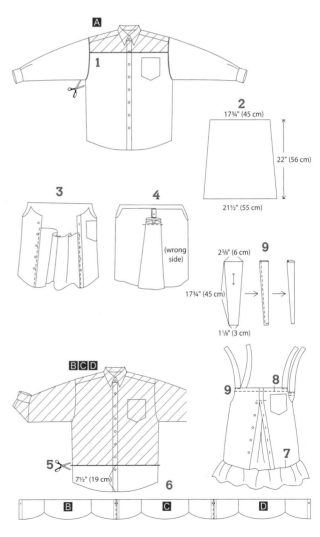

MATERIALS

4 shirts **(Men's L)**
23½" (60 cm)–long elastic tape [1" (2.5 cm) wide]

A   B   C   D

INSTRUCTIONS

1. Cut shirt A. This will become the bodice.

2. Cut a trapezoidal piece from each sleeve. With right sides together, sew trapezoids together along the 22" (56 cm) edge. Eventually, this will become the front pleat.

3. Align the bottom edge of the pleat piece with the bottom edge of front placket and topstitch to make a tube.

4. Fasten the top button and fold the pleats (see illustration 4). On the wrong side, stitch across the pleats to secure.

5. Cut shirts B, C, and D.

6. Attach the pieces by overlapping and topstitching at each placket to create a band. This will become the ruffled hem.

7. Sew gathering seams on the top edge of the ruffled hem. Adjust gathers to fit the bottom edge of piece A and sew with right sides together.

8. Fold the top raw edge of the bodice front and back over twice and stitch. Thread elastic tape through (see page 87) and gather until the finished width of the front bodice is 11" (28 cm) and the back bodice is 10¼" (26 cm). Sew the opening closed at the ends, making sure to stitch through elastic tape.

9. Make four straps from the remaining fabric and sew in place to finish the top.

Blouse with Kimono Sleeves

from **Men's Shirts,** *Shown on page 37*

MATERIALS

2 shirts (**Men's L**)

$19\frac{3}{4}$" (50 cm)–long elastic tape [$\frac{3}{8}$" (0.8 cm) wide]

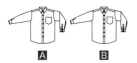

INSTRUCTIONS

1. Cut the bodice front and back of shirt A. This will become the blouse bodice. Cut off the collar and collar band.

2. Fold the top raw edge of the bodice front over twice and stitch, leaving an opening for the elastic tape. Thread elastic tape through and gather the fabric until the finished width is $7\frac{3}{4}$" (20 cm). Secure in place (see page 87). Repeat the process for the back.

3. With shirt B buttoned, cut the bodice front and back. With right sides together, sew the shorter sides to create two tubes. These will become the sleeves. Cut off the collar and collar band.

4. Attach the sleeves to the bodice with the button placket positioned at the top of the sleeve. Sew the underarm portion of the sleeve.

5. Using a hand-sewing needle and thread, gather the remaining portion of each sleeve until it is the same length as the collar band.

6. Sew the collars to the remaining portion of each sleeve (see illustration 6).

7. Fold the raw edge of sleeve openings over twice and stitch to create a finished sleeve.

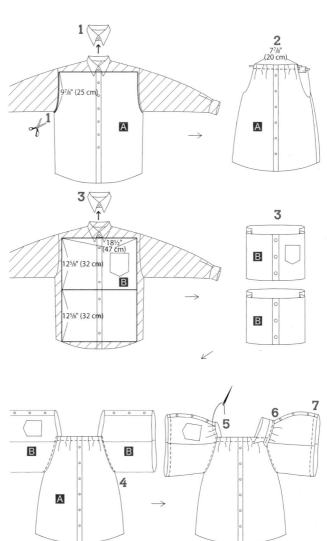

You will only need two men's shirts to make this blouse. For more color, incorporate fabrics from an additional shirt or two.

Two-Way Strapless Dress from Men's Shirts

The button placket and buttons are the unsung heroes of this tube dress. If you fold up the placket hem (with the original buttons) this dress converts into a miniskirt.

Instructions, page 42

Two-Way Strapless Dress

from Men's Shirts, *Shown on page 40*

MATERIALS

2 to 3 shirts **(Men's XL)**

About 27½" (70 cm)–long elastic tape [⅝" (1.5 cm) wide]

INSTRUCTIONS

1. Cut a 9" (23 cm)–wide rectangle from the right front bodice (the side with buttons) of all three shirts. With right sides together, sew the cut pieces into a 39¼" (100 cm)–long tube.

2. Cut the center front button placket from two of the shirts. With right sides together, sew the cut pieces into a 47¼" (120 cm) loop.

3. Cut a 17¾" (45 cm)–wide rectangle from the bodice back of all three shirts. With right sides together, sew cut pieces into a 78¾" (200 cm)–long tube. Sew gathering seams onto both top and bottom edges (see page 87).

4. Adjust gathers to fit. With right sides together, sew the top edge of the piece from step 3 to the buttoned edge of the piece from step 1.

5. Adjust gathers to fit. With right sides together, sew the bottom edge of piece from step 3 to the piece from step 2.

6. Fold the top raw edge of garment over twice and stitch, leaving an opening for the elastic tape. Thread elastic tape through, secure in place, and sew the opening closed to finish (see page 87).

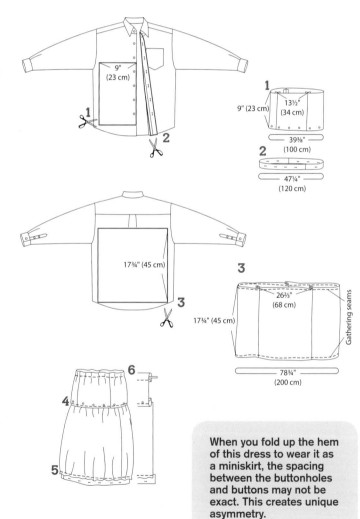

When you fold up the hem of this dress to wear it as a miniskirt, the spacing between the buttonholes and buttons may not be exact. This creates unique asymmetry.

Raglan T-shirt
<u>with</u> **Men's Shirts Sleeves,** *Shown on page 68*

MATERIALS

1 shirt **(Men's XL)**

1 T-shirt **(Women's S)** (For a larger-sized finished garment, begin with a larger-sized women's T-shirt)

15¾" (40 cm)–long elastic tape [¼" (0.7 cm) wide]

INSTRUCTIONS

1. Cut off the shirt sleeves.

2. Cut off the shirt cuffs. Fold the raw edges over twice and stitch, leaving an opening for the elastic tape. Thread the elastic tape through, secure in place, and sew the opening closed (see page 87).

3. Cut off the T-shirt sleeves.

4. Sew two rows of gathering stitches along the underarm of the shirt sleeves. With right sides together, sew the shirt sleeves to the T-shirt bodice by aligning them at the top shoulder. The garment is finished.

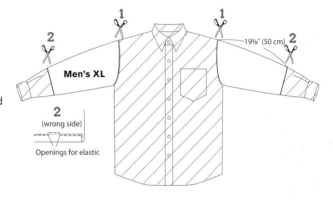

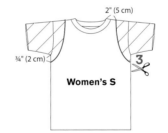

Six-Sleeved Dress
from Men's Shirts

This dress' six sleeves bloom from two collarless shirts grafted to a third shirt. Fine woven cotton shirts are ideal for this dress because of their polished finish and elegant drape.

Instructions, page 46

Gilet
<u>from</u> Men's Shirts

The shirt's placket curves into a natural (and clever) neckline for this gilet. The wide shoulder evokes a French sleeve, and it is perfect for additional lace details.

Instructions, page 47

Six-Sleeved Dress

from Men's Shirts, *Shown on page 44*

MATERIALS

3 shirts **(Men's L)**

INSTRUCTIONS

1. Cut the bodice, collar, center front button placket, and sleeves of shirt A.

2. Fold the raw edges of the center front over twice and stitch. Continue stitching around the neck without folding the raw edges. This will become the dress bodice.

3. Cut shirts B and C horizontally from shoulder seams and at sleeve button plackets.

4. Attach shirts B and C by buttoning them together. Sew gathering seams at the top edge (see page 87).

5. Adjust the gathers to fit. With right sides together, sew the bottom raw edge of the piece from step 2 to the gathered top edge of the piece from step 4.

6. Attach four even lengths of twill tape (see illustration 6).

> To finish the sleeves, simply roll them up to their desired length, or for a more finished look, fold the raw edges over twice and stitch.

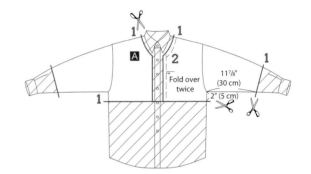

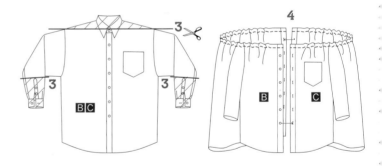

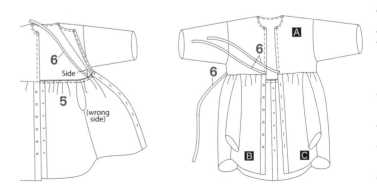

Gilet

from **Men's Shirts,** *Shown on page 45*

MATERIALS

1 shirt **(Men's XL)**

Fringed trim: length of center front placket + ¾" (2 cm) long (2 pieces)

INSTRUCTIONS

1. Cut off the collar, leaving the collar band attached to the shirt.

2. Cut off the sleeves, leaving ⅜" (1 cm) fabric at the armhole.

3. Cut open both side seams.

4. Working with the back bodice only, cut the yoke.

5. Starting at the bottom hem, trim the front bodice at each side until it aligns with armhole (see illustration 5).

6. Stitch the fringed trim onto each side of the button placket.

7. Fasten the top button, overlap the collar band, and stitch the neck opening closed (see illustration 7).

8. With right sides together, align the edge of the back yoke (A) with the edge of the front bodice (a) and sew a 5" (13 cm) seam (see illustration 8). Repeat the process with (B) and (b).

9. Fold the raw edges of the armhole over twice and stitch to finish the sleeve.

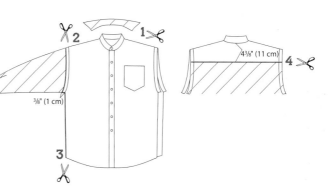

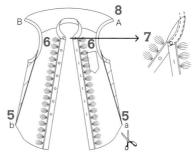

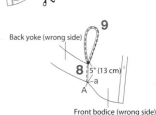

> Make sure you choose a shirt that has a back yoke to maximize the draped effect of the gilet.

Swinging Halter Top from Men's Shirt Front

This top is a marvel of efficiency—it uses only the front part of a men's shirt. The placket, button, and cuffs add clever style to the top edging. For all its femininity, it still retains the spirit of a man's shirt.

Instructions, page 50

Sleeveless Blouse
from Men's Shirt

This summery blouse is made from a shirt
with its collar and sleeves removed. Use
colorful ribbons in contrasting fabrics, play
with scraps left over from other projects,
or dress up the sash with a silk scarf.

Instructions, page 51

49

Swinging Halter Top

<u>from</u> **Men's Shirt Front,** *Shown on page 48*

MATERIALS

1 shirt **(Men's XL)**

15¾" (40 cm)–long elastic tape [¼" (0.7 cm) wide]

INSTRUCTIONS

1. Cut a rectangle from the side of the front bodice with buttonholes. Note that the rectangle may extend onto part of the sleeve and back bodice. This will become the front bodice.

2. Sew darts.

3. Cut off the center front button placket and stitch along the raw edge. This will become the halter strap.

4. Cut a rectangle from the side of the front bodice that originally had buttons. This will become the back bodice.

5. Fold one of the long raw edges of the piece made in step 4 over twice and stitch. Thread elastic tape through (see page 87) and gather until the finished width is 13¾" (35 cm). Stitch through elastic tape at left edge to secure in place. Starting at the top left and stopping at the bottom right, fold the raw edge over twice and stitch (see illustration 5).

6. With right sides together, sew the front and back bodices together along the right side only. Make sure to stitch through the elastic tape to secure it in place.

7. Cut off a 2" (5 cm) piece of the sleeve cuff with a buttonhole and sew it to the top left edge of the front bodice. Remove the coordinating button from the cuff and attach it to the top left edge of the back bodice.

8. Attach the halter strap to the front bodice by buttoning at desired length.

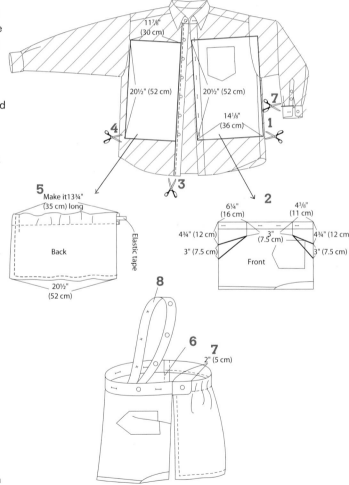

Sleeveless Blouse

from **Men's Shirt,** *Shown on page 49*

MATERIALS

1 shirt **(Men's L)**
Coordinating fabric 23½" x 23½" (60 x 60 cm)
86½" (220 cm)–long bias tape [⅜" (1 cm) wide]

INSTRUCTIONS

1. Cut the sleeves and neck line.

2. Wrap the sleeve and neck openings with bias tape. Stitch close to the edge of the top fold of the bias tape, making sure to catch the bottom fold with the needle while sewing.

3. Make four ribbons from coordinating fabric (see illustration 3).

4. Attach the ribbons to the shirt at each sleeve opening. Use the ribbons to tie bows at both the front and the back.

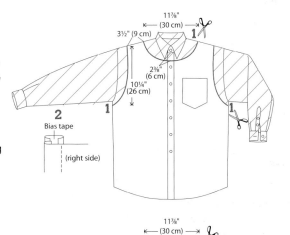

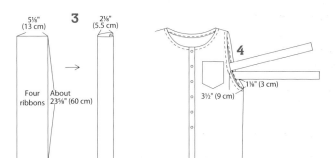

Halter Top
<u>from</u> Men's Shirt

This halter top is crafted from nearly the
entire body of the shirt. By shifting the
shirts from back to front, the front placket
morphs into a center back detail.

Instructions, page 54

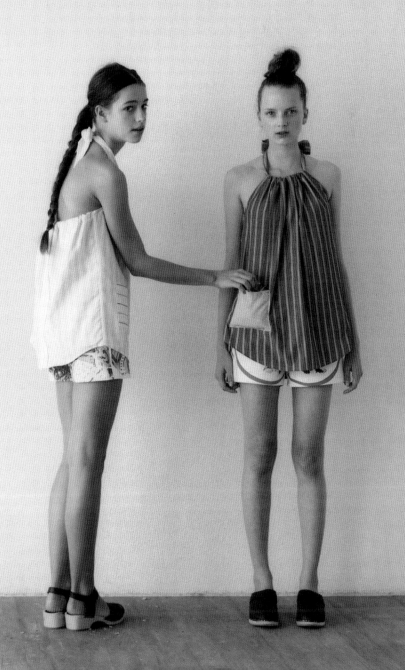

Halter Top

from **Men's Shirt,** *Shown on page 52*

MATERIALS

1 shirt **(Men's L)**
Coordinating fabric 7¼" x 7¼" (20 x 20 cm)
15¾" (40 cm)–long elastic tape [¼" (0.7 cm) wide]

INSTRUCTIONS

1. Cut the front and back bodice individually (see illustration 1).

2. On the back bodice, fold the raw edge of the armhole over twice and stitch.

3. With the shirt buttoned, fold the top raw edge of front bodice over twice and stitch. Thread elastic tape through and sew one end in place. Gather until the finished width is 13¾" (35 cm). Secure the elastic in place and sew the opening closed (see page 87).

4. Fold the top raw edge of the back bodice over twice and stitch, leaving an opening wide enough for the strap. This will become the front bodice of the finished halter top.

5. Make a pocket from the coordinating fabric and sew it onto the halter top.

6. Using the remaining sleeve fabric, make a strap (see illustration 6) and thread it though the opening.

> You can use extra shirt fabric from this project to make the pocket or use a contrasting fabric for a more playful look.

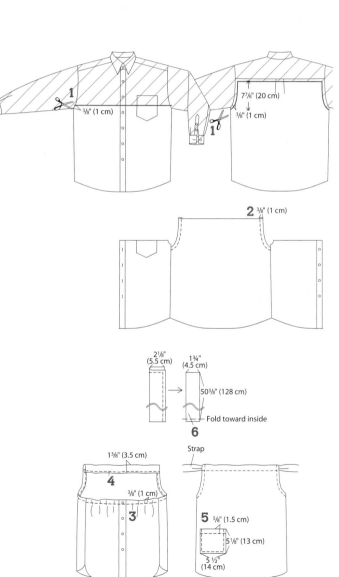

Crazy Collars Tote Bag

from **Men's Shirts,** *Shown on page 68*

MATERIALS

13 shirt collars (including collar bands)
Fabric 9¾" x 11¾" (25 x 30 cm)

INSTRUCTIONS

1. Overlap the collars (with collar bands) ⅜" (1 cm) and stitch. Make two "columns" of six collars each. Sew the columns into a tube.

2. Cut the piece of fabric into an oval using the dimensions in the diagram below. With right sides together, sew the oval to the piece from step 1 to make the bag bottom.

3. Sew another collar to the bag to make a handle.

> **For a smaller version of the bag, make two columns of three collars each.**

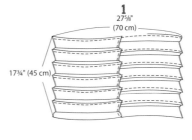

1
27⅝"
(70 cm)

17¾" (45 cm)

7⅞"
(20 cm)

11"
(28 cm)

Bag bottom

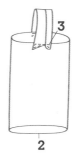

3

2

Long Jumper
from Layered Men's Shirts

This piece is made by sewing two shirts lengthwise, one stacked on top of another, piggy-back style. Thick, durable weekend shirts are better suited to this design than fine-woven dress shirts.

Instructions, page 58

High-Waisted Blouse
<u>from</u> Men's Shirts

Gather all ye oversized shirts! Careful measurements are key to making this blouse from two different pieces. The center front placket evolves into a belt.

Instructions, page 59

Long Jumper

<u>from</u> **Layered Men's Shirts,** *Shown on page 56*

MATERIALS

2 shirts **(Men's XL)**

23½" (60 cm)–long elastic tape [¼" (0.7 cm) wide]

INSTRUCTIONS

1. Cut the neckline of shirt A. Fold the raw edge over twice and stitch, leaving an opening for the elastic tape. Thread the elastic tape through, secure in place, and sew the opening closed (see page 87).

2. Cut off the sleeves 11" (28 cm) from the neckline.

3. Cut the sleeve cuffs ⅜" (1 cm) from the sleeve button placket.

4. Sew gathering seams on the sleeve openings. Adjust the gathers to fit the sleeve cuffs. With right sides together, sew the sleeve cuffs onto the sleeve openings.

5. On shirt B, cut the sleeve ⅜" (1 cm) from the armhole and cut 26 ¾" (68 cm) from the bottom. Repeat cuts on the back.

6. Fold the raw edge of shirt B over and overlap it with shirt A. Sew shirts A and B together (see illustration 6) to finish the dress.

> If you are using two different-sized shirts, use the bigger one as shirt B and gather it under the armholes to achieve desired size.

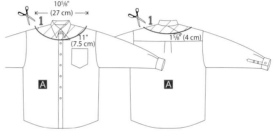

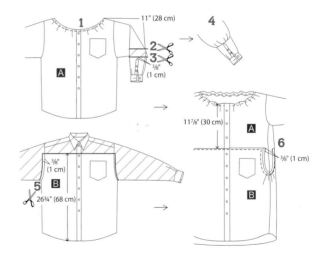

High-Waisted Blouse
from Men's Shirts, *Shown on page 57*

MATERIALS

2 shirts **(Men's L)**
23 ½" (60 cm)–long elastic tape [¼" (0.7 cm) wide]

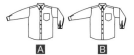

INSTRUCTIONS

1. With shirt A buttoned, cut the button placket.

2. Cut horizontally 14¼" (36 cm) from the center bottom of the shirt, cutting through both front and back layers.

3. Starting on the front and continuing on the back, cut the neck (see illustration 3).

4. Cut a rectangle from the center back. With right sides together, sew the raw edges together to create the shirt bodice.

5. Using the piece of shirt A from step 2, cut open the back, starting at the center bottom.

6. With shirt B buttoned, cut the front bodice.

7. With right sides together, align the bottom of shirt A from step 5 with the bottom of shirt B from 6 and sew together (see illustration 7). This will become the skirt.

8. Sew gathering seams across the top raw edge of the skirt and adjust gathers to fit shirt bodice.

9. Overlap the skirt with the bodice and sew together.

10. Fold the raw edges at center front and neck over twice and stitch.

11. Cut the sleeves at the sleeve plackets. Fold the raw edges over twice and stitch, leaving an opening for the elastic tape. Thread the elastic tape through, secure in place, and sew the opening closed (see page 87).

12. Attach the front button placket and button strip cut in step 1 by fastening one button and stitching. This will become the belt.

13. Position the belt around the waist with the button portion on the right side of the bodice. Attach the belt to the garment by stitching it in place.

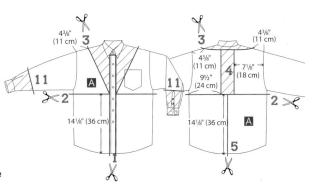

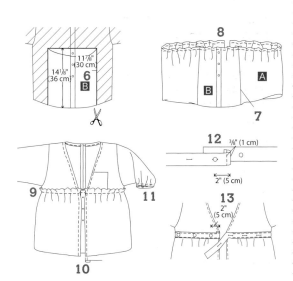

Patched Blouse
<u>with</u> Men's Shirt Cuff

This blouse is made by pleating the shirt
at the center and patching it with a cuff.
Adjust the length of the sleeves as you
wish, rolling up your sleeves to get down
to business.

Instructions, page 62

Cross-Front Halter Top <u>from</u> Men's Shirt

The button placket wraps around this piece in one design line from the front edge to the halter neck. A fine-woven dress shirt is ideal for this top.

Instructions, page 63

Patched Blouse
<u>with</u> **Men's Shirt Cuff,** *Shown on page 60*

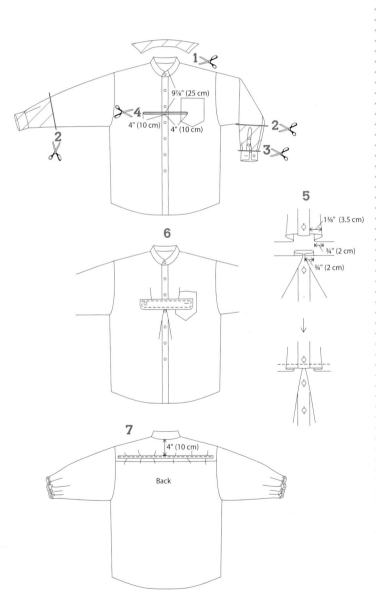

MATERIALS

1 shirt **(Men's L)**

37½" (95 cm)–long elastic tape [¼" (0.7 cm) wide]

INSTRUCTIONS

1. Cut off the collar, leaving the collar band on the shirt.

2. Cut the sleeves at the sleeve plackets. Fold the raw edges over twice and stitch, leaving an opening for the elastic tape. Thread 11¾" (30 cm) of the tape through each sleeve, secure in place, and sew the opening closed (see page 87).

3. Remove the cuff from one sleeve.

4. With the shirt buttoned, make a horizontal cut across the middle.

5. Fold pleats above and below the cut (see illustration 5). Overlap the cut edges and stitch, securing pleats in place.

6. Position the cuff on top of pleats and topstitch to the shirt.

7. Attach the remaining elastic tape to the wrong side of the back bodice to finish.

Cross-Front Halter Top

from **Men's Shirt,** *Shown on page 61*

MATERIALS

1 shirt **(Men's L)**

INSTRUCTIONS

1. With the shirt buttoned, cut out the center front button placket.

2. Working with both layers, cut the front bodice and the back bodice continuously.

3. With right sides together, sew the center front raw edges together.

4. On both the front and back, fold the top corners to the inside and stitch (see illustration 4). On the front, fold a pleat at the center front.

5. Fasten the second to last button on the button placket. Align the button placket at center front and topstitch onto shirt along the fold line. Adjust the halter strap to desired length, fasten button, and topstitch to center back to finish.

> After attaching the halter strap to the shirt front, try it on and adjust the strap length to fit your body before sewing it to the back.

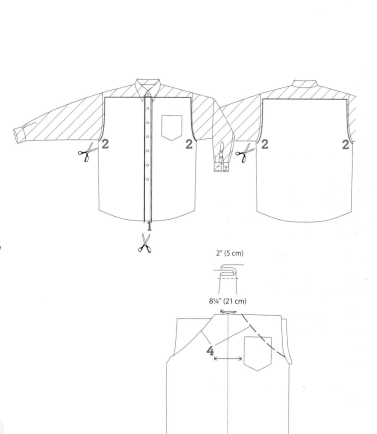

Arm-in-Arm Skirt
from Men's Shirts

This skirt is built from two "aprons" buttoned together. Be sure to use shirts with yokes to make the most of the design. The width or the length of the yokes does not need to be the same. The more they differ, the more asymmetry you'll incorporate.

Instructions, page 66

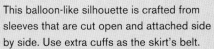

Balloon Skirt
<u>from</u> Men's Shirt Sleeves

This balloon-like silhouette is crafted from
sleeves that are cut open and attached side
by side. Use extra cuffs as the skirt's belt.

Instructions, page 67

Arm-in-Arm Skirt
from **Men's Shirts,** *Shown on page 64*

MATERIALS

2 shirts **(Men's XL)**

2 ¼ yards (200 cm) twill tape [⅜" (1 cm) wide]

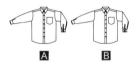

INSTRUCTIONS

1. Cut the yoke of shirt A by cutting shoulder, armhole, and neck seams.

2. Fold the cut piece of fabric into a rectangle, so the neck curves are hidden. This will become the belt.

3. Cut the remaining bodice of shirt A. This will become the skirt.

4. Cut the sleeves. Working with the cut off portion of the sleeves, fold the raw edges over twice and stitch. Remove the buttons from the sleeve cuffs. These will become the apron ties.

5. Turn one armhole opening inside out and sew the end closed. Turn it right side out and tuck it into the armhole to create a pocket. Repeat the process for the other armhole.

6. Sew gathering seams at the top of the skirt. Adjust to the width of the belt. Sew the belt onto the skirt.

7. Attach the apron ties by sewing a sleeve cuff onto each end of the belt.

8. Follow the same process to make another skirt from shirt B. For the apron ties, use twill tape instead of sleeve fabric. Button the two skirts together at the sides to finish.

> Be sure to use two shirts that each have a yoke. Both shirts should have have the same button spacing. To wear the skirt, tie the twill tape from skirt B in front and the sleeve ties from skirt A in the back.

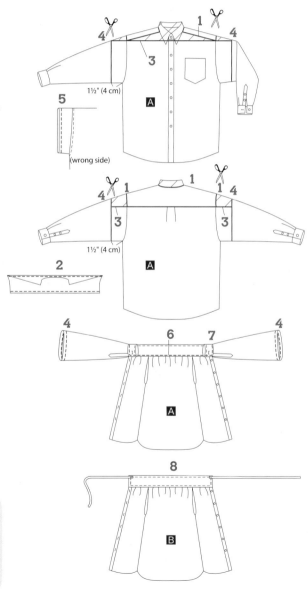

Balloon Skirt
from **Men's Shirt Sleeves,** *Shown on page 65*

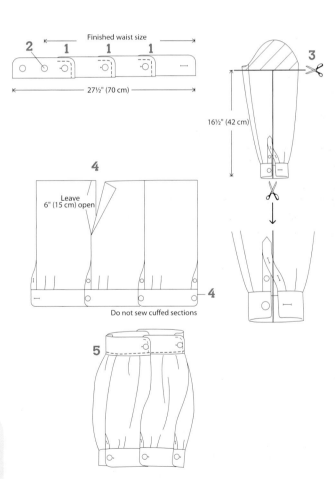

MATERIALS

5 shirts **(Men's, any size)**

INSTRUCTIONS

1. Cut the cuffs of shirts A, B, C, and D, overlap them, and stitch them together. Make sure to use sleeve cuffs cut from the same side of the shirt (either right or left). This will become the waistband.

2. Attach a button to the point where the waistband will fasten on the finished skirt.

3. Remove the buttons on the remaining sleeves of shirts A, B, C, D, and E and cut open the sleeves, making sure to cut through top layer only. Make a horizontal cut across the top of the sleeves.

4. With right sides together, sew five sleeves together to create the skirt. Do not stitch the cuffed sections at the bottom. Instead, use buttons to connect them. Leave one 6" (15 cm) area open (see illustration 4).

5. Gather the top edge of the skirt to make it fit the waistband. Stitch the waistband onto the skirt to finish.

> You need five whole shirts to make this skirt since it calls for the same sleeve from each shirt, but you can create a second skirt from the remaining sleeves.

Raglan T-shirt
<u>with</u> Men's Shirt Sleeves

A T-shirt marriage made in heaven. Just attach shirt sleeves to your favorite tee for simple, clever style.

Instructions, page 43

Crazy Collars Tote Bag
from Men's Shirts

How many fashion perps have you collared
lately? This bag is made from piles of actual
collars from men's dress shirts—as many as
13, but you can make a smaller version.

Instructions, page 55

Scarves <u>and</u> Necktles ▶ ▶ ▶ ▶ ▶ ▶ ▶ ▶ ▶

Among the rare accessories men have in their fashion arsenal, scarves and neckties are essential gear. Beyond their versatility, their wide variety of color, fabrics, and textures makes them perfect for crafting and refashioning. When sewing, you don't need to worry about folding and hemming their edges, so they are ideal for beginners.

Vest
<u>from</u> Two Scarves

A simple scarf draped around the neck becomes the collar and front of the body, and a second scarf becomes the back. The fringe along the bottom edge is an optional design accent. Play with the details in your own scarves.

Instructions, page 74

Vest

from **Two Scarves,** *Shown on page 72*

MATERIALS

2 fringed scarves [about 11¾" x 59" (30 x 150 cm) without fringe]

INSTRUCTIONS

1. Cut off the fringe sections and cut the ends of scarf A at an angle.

2. Cut one fringe section (from step 1) in half and sew onto the right side of scarf B. (This step creates faux pockets. Functioning pockets can be created by repositioning the seams.)

3. With right sides together, align the other fringe section with the center of scarf B and sew.

4. With right sides together, align ♥ (heart symbols) on each scarf and sew.

5. Sew gathering seams on the inside center edge of scarf A. Adjust gathers to fit the size of ★ (star symbol) on scarf B. Sew scarves A and B together to finish.

The two scarves don't need to be the same length. If you are using two scarves of different lengths, use the shorter one as scarf A and adjust step 5 instructions accordingly.

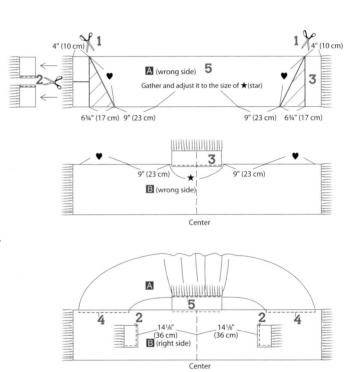

Blouse

<u>with</u> Necktie, *Shown on page 84*

MATERIALS

1 long-sleeve sweatshirt **(Men's L)**

1 necktie

23 ½" (60 cm)–long elastic tape [¼" (0.7 cm) wide]

INSTRUCTIONS

1. Cut the sweatshirt sleeves. Fold the raw edges over twice and stitch, leaving an opening for the elastic tape. Thread the elastic tape through, secure in place, and sew the opening closed (see page 87).

2. Cut the bottom edge of the shirt. Fold the raw edge over twice and stitch.

3. Align the center of the tie with the center back of the sweatshirt. Topstitch the tie to the ribbed neckline of the sweatshirt. Leave the tie unattached at the center front.

When attaching the tie, make sure to backstitch at the ends of the seams to secure the tie.

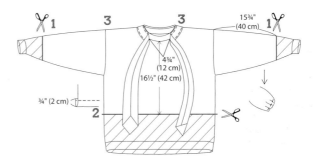

15¾" (40 cm)

4¾" (12 cm)

16½" (42 cm)

¾" (2 cm)

Two-Way Poncho/Skirt
<u>from</u> **Scarves**

Collect all the extra, mismatched, well-loved scarves you have at home. Since the poncho/skirt is built by aligning them on one side and then cutting them to size, the dimensions of the scarves don't matter. This piece is a super-warm addition to your cool-weather wardrobe.

Instructions, page 78

Two-Way Poncho/Skirt

from Scarves, *Shown on page 76*

MATERIALS

3 fringed scarves [about 11¾" x 59" (30 x 150 cm) without fringe]
67" (170 cm)–long string

INSTRUCTIONS

1. Cut all three scarves 18¾" (48 cm) from each end (measure from the base of the fringe).

2. Overlap each scarf section ⅜" (1 cm) along the sides and sew together. For the center front seam only, sew with right sides together.

3. Cut openings for the string.

4. Fold the top raw edge over 1¼" (3 cm) and stitch.

5. Thread the string through to finish.

The skirt length used in these instructions is only a suggestion. For a longer skirt, cut the scarves into longer sections in step 1. For best results, start with scarves that are at least 38¼" (100cm) long.

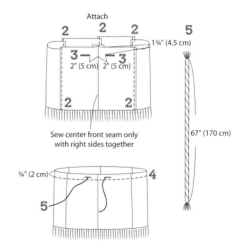

Sew center front seam only with right sides together

Hold Me Tie!

with Necktie, *Shown on page 85*

MATERIALS

1 long-sleeve sweatshirt **(Men's L)**
1 necktie
7" (18 cm)–long elastic tape [1" (2.5 cm) wide]

INSTRUCTIONS

1. Cut the necktie in half.

2. Attach the necktie sections to the sweatshirt at the shoulders. First, sew the tie to the back of the sweatshirt, just below the shoulder seam, with the wrong side of the tie facing up. Then, flip the tie to the front of the sweatshirt and sew along the shoulder seam to secure it in place.

3. Cut off the sleeves 10½" (27 cm) from the shoulder. Cut the separated sleeve cuff sections 5" (13 cm) from the bottom edge of the cuff. Sew gathering seams on the sleeve openings. Adjust gathers to fit sleeve cuff sections. With right sides together, sew sleeve cuff sections onto sleeve openings.

4. Stretch the elastic tape to 9¾" (25 cm) and sew it to the center back on the wrong side of the sweatshirt to finish.

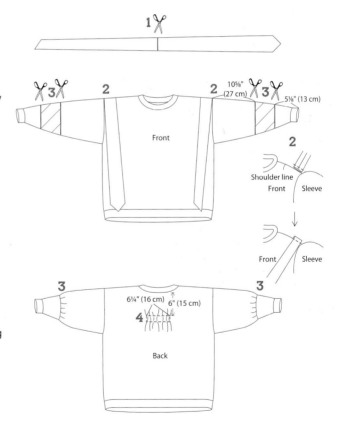

79

Poncho
from Four Scarves

The transformation of scarves into ponchos is absurdly simple. Just sew two sets of scarves that are the same length at the shoulder and part of the bottom edge. Any combination of patterns will do, but be sure to choose patterns around the neckline that match your face. Another perk: the poncho is 100% reversible.

Instructions, page 82

Mini Poncho
from Two Scarves

You can also wear this poncho as a shrug by slipping your arms through it.

Instructions, page 83

Poncho

<u>from</u> **Four Scarves,** *Shown on page 80*

MATERIALS

4 fringed scarves [about 11¾" x 59" (30 x 150 cm) without fringe]

INSTRUCTIONS

1. Overlap scarves A and B ⅜" (1 cm) along the long edge and sew. Repeat the process for scarves C and D.

2. With right sides together, sew scarves A and C along the long edge, leaving a 15¾" (40 cm) opening at the center. This will become the neck opening.

3. Topstitch the neck opening.

4. On the right side of poncho, stitch 15¾" (40 cm) in from each edge, making sure to stitch through both layers.

The four scarves don't need to be the same length. If your scarves are different lengths, follow these additional instructions: For steps 1 and 2, align the center of each scarf and sew together. For step 4, sew 15¾" (40 cm) in from the edge of the longer scarf.

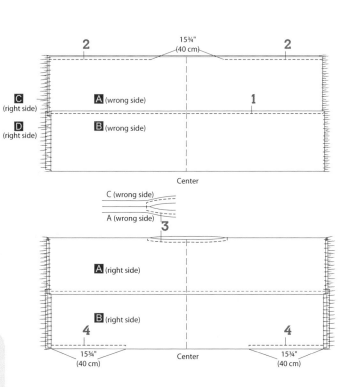

Mini Poncho

<u>from</u> **Two Scarves,** *Shown on page 81*

MATERIALS

2 fringed scarves [about 11¾" x 59" (30 x 150 cm) without fringe]

INSTRUCTIONS

1. With right sides together, sew scarves A and B along their long edges, leaving a 15¾" (40 cm) opening at the center. This will become the neck opening.

2. Topstitch the neck opening.

3. On the right side of the poncho, stitch 15¾" (40 cm) in from each edge, making sure to stitch through both layers.

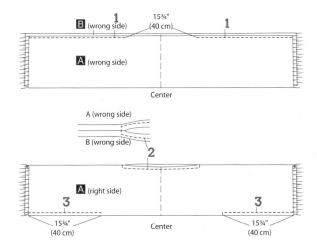

The two scarves don't need to be the same length. If your scarves are different lengths, follow these additional instructions: For step 1, align the center of each scarf and sew together. For step 3, sew 15¾" (40 cm) in from the edge of the longer scarf.

Blouse
<u>with</u> Necktie

This blouse is inspired by the image of a businessman who has loosened his tie at the end of a long day. The construction is simple: just sew a necktie to the neckline of a sweatshirt.

Instructions, page 75

Hold Me Tie!
<u>with</u> Necktie

Cut a necktie in half and sew both pieces to the shoulder of a sweatshirt. No one expects to see a tie in women's fashion. Surprise and charm the masses!

Instructions, page 79

Strapless Top with Bow

from **Sweatshirt,** *Shown on page 33*

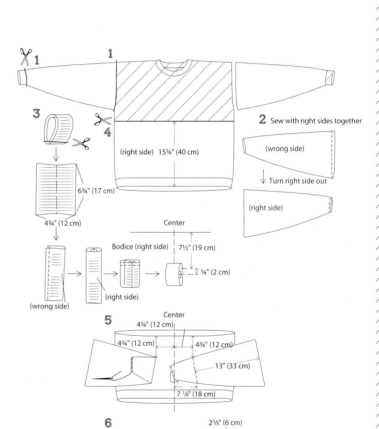

MATERIALS

1 long-sleeve sweatshirt **(Men's XL)**

27½" (70 cm)–long elastic tape [1" (2.5 cm) wide]

INSTRUCTIONS

1. Cut the sleeves and cuffs from the sweatshirt.

2. With right sides together, sew the armhole ends of the sleeves closed. Turn the sleeves right side out, fold the cuff ends to the inside, and topstitch around the openings.

3. Make a band from one ribbed cuff.

4. Cut the sweatshirt bodice.

5. Sew the sleeves and band to the bodice (see illustration 5). Fold the narrow sleeve ends back and hemstitch to the wider sections of the sleeves, being careful not to stitch through to the bodice.

6. Fold the top raw edge of the bodice over and sew, leaving an opening for the elastic tape. Thread the elastic tape through, secure in place, and sew the opening closed (see page 87). Thread the wide sleeve ends through the band to finish.

Sewing Guide

Finishing Fabric Edges

Making a Single-Fold Hem

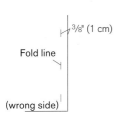

³⁄₈" (1 cm)

Fold line

(wrong side)

1. Fold raw edge over ³⁄₈" (1 cm). Press.

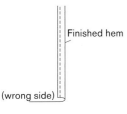

Finished hem

(wrong side)

2. Stitch along folded edge.

Making a Double-Fold Hem

Fold line

(wrong side)

1. Fold raw edge over ³⁄₈" (1 cm). Press.

(wrong side)

Finished hem

2. Fold over ³⁄₈" (1 cm) again. Press.

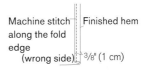

Machine stitch along the fold edge

Finished hem

(wrong side)   ³⁄₈" (1 cm)

3. Stitch along folded edge.

Using Elastic Tape

Gathering Using Elastic Thread

* When threading the machine, gently hand wind the elastic thread around the bobbin. Use regular machine thread for the top thread.
* The amount of gathers changes depending on the width of the stitch—wider stitches create more gathers. Try some sample stitches first and then adjust the width to achieve the desired results.

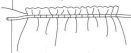

Machine thread (top thread)

Elastic thread (bottom thread)

1. Stitch with the bobbin thread seam on the wrong side of the fabric.

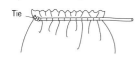

Tie

2. Knot the tail of the elastic thread. Pull the elastic thread and adjust gathers to the desired finished size.

Threading Elastic Tape Through Opening

1. Sew a casing wide enough for the elastic tape by folding the raw edges over twice and stitching close to the fold. Leave an opening about 2" (5 cm) wide.

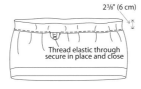

2³⁄₈" (6 cm)

Thread elastic through secure in place and close

2. Thread the elastic tape through, secure in place, and sew the opening closed.

Securing Elastic Tape

Sew one end

(wrong side)

1. Thread the elastic tape through and sew one end in place.

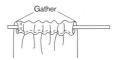

Gather

2. Gather the tape to the finished size.

Sew other end

3. Sew the other end of the elastic tape in place.

Sizing Guide

As *Cut-Up Couture* uses existing garments as material for creating new styles, the designs included in this book are one-size-fits-most. To customize the fit, simply start with smaller or larger T-shirts, sweatshirts, and dress shirts based on your needs. Use the measurements provided below as a guide when selecting your materials in order to achieve the best-fitting finished garment.

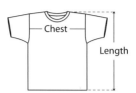

Men's T-Shirt

Size	Chest	Length
Small (S)	34"-36" (86.5-91.5 cm)	28" (71 cm)
Medium (M)	38"-40" (96.5-101.5 cm)	29" (73.5 cm)
Large (L)	42"-44" (106.5-112 cm)	30" (76 cm)
Extra Large (XL)	46"-48" (117-122 cm)	31" (78.5 cm)
Extra Extra Large (2XL)	50"-52" (127-132 cm)	32" (81.5 cm)

Men's Sweatshirt

Size	Chest	Length
Small (S)	34"-36" (86.5-91.5 cm)	28" (71 cm)
Medium (M)	38"-40" (96.5-101.5 cm)	29" (73.5 cm)
Large (L)	42"-44" (106.5-112 cm)	30" (76 cm)
Extra Large (XL)	46"-48" (117-122 cm)	31" (78.5 cm)
Extra Extra Large (2XL)	50"-52" (127-132 cm)	32" (81.5 cm)

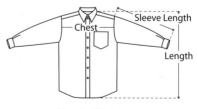

Men's Shirt

Size	Chest	Length	Sleeve Length
Small (S)	34"-36" (86.5-91.5 cm)	28" (71 cm)	32"-33" (81.5-84 cm)
Medium (M)	38"-40" (96.5-101.5 cm)	29" (73.5 cm)	33"-34" (84-86.5 cm)
Large (L)	42"-44" (106.5-112 cm)	30" (76 cm)	34"-35" (86.5-89 cm)
Extra Large (XL)	46"-48" (117-122 cm)	31" (78.5 cm)	35"-36" (89-91.5 cm)
Extra Extra Large (2XL)	50"-52" (127-132 cm)	32" (81.5 cm)	36"-37" (91.5-94 cm)